A Note from
Mary Pope Osborne About the

When I write Magic Tree House® adventures, I love including facts about the times and places Jack and Annie visit. But when readers finish these adventures, I want them to learn even more. So that's why we write a series of nonfiction books that are companions to the fiction titles in the Magic Tree House® series. We call these books Fact Trackers because we love to track the facts! Whether we're researching dinosaurs, pyramids, Pilgrims, sea monsters, or cobras, we're always amazed at how wondrous and surprising the real world is. We want you to experience the same wonder we do—so get out your pencils and notebooks and hit the trail with us. You can be a Magic Tree House® Fact Tracker, too!

Here's what kids, parents, and teachers have to say about the Magic Tree House® Fact Trackers:

"They are so good. I can't wait for the next one. All I can say for now is prepare to be amazed!" —Alexander N.

"I have read every Magic Tree House book there is. The [Fact Trackers] are a thrilling way to get more information about the special events in the story." —John R.

"These are fascinating nonfiction books that enhance the magical time-traveling adventures of Jack and Annie. I love these books, especially *American Revolution*. I was learning so much, and I didn't even know it!" —Tori Beth S.

"[They] are an excellent 'behind-the-scenes' look at what the [Magic Tree House fiction] has started in your imagination! You can't buy one without the other; they are such a complement to one another." —Erika N., mom

"Magic Tree House [Fact Trackers] took my children on a journey from Frog Creek, Pennsylvania, to so many significant historical events! The detailed manuals are a remarkable addition to the classic fiction Magic Tree House books we adore!" —Jenny S., mom

"[They] are very useful tools in my classroom, as they allow for students to be part of the planning process. Together, we find facts in the [Fact Trackers] to extend the learning introduced in the fictional companions. Researching and planning classroom activities, such as our class Olympics based on facts found in *Ancient Greece and the Olympics*, help create a genuine love for learning!" —Paula H., teacher

MAGIC TREE HOUSE® FACT TRACKER

Space

A NONFICTION COMPANION TO MAGIC TREE HOUSE #8:
Midnight on the Moon

BY WILL OSBORNE
AND MARY POPE OSBORNE

ILLUSTRATED BY SAL MURDOCCA

A STEPPING STONE BOOK™
Random House 🏠 New York

Text copyright © 2002 by Will Osborne and Mary Pope Osborne
Illustrations copyright © 2002 by Sal Murdocca
Cover photograph copyright © Space Telescope Science Institute/NASA/
Science Photo Library

The Magic Tree House Fact Tracker series was formerly known
as the Magic Tree House Research Guide series.

Visit us on the Web!
MagicTreeHouse.com
randomhousekids.com

Educators and librarians, for a variety of teaching tools, visit us at
RHTeachersLibrarians.com

Library of Congress Cataloging-in-Publication Data
Osborne, Will.
Space : a nonfiction companion to Magic tree house #8, Midnight on the moon /
by Will Osborne and Mary Pope Osborne ; illustrated by Sal Murdocca.
    p.   cm. — (Magic tree house fact tracker)
"A Stepping Stone book."
Includes index.
ISBN 978-0-375-81356-6 (trade) — ISBN 978-0-375-91356-3 (lib. bdg.) —
ISBN 978-0-307-97518-8 (ebook)
1. Astronomy—Juvenile literature. 2. Space flight—Juvenile literature.
I. Osborne, Mary Pope. II. Murdocca, Sal, ill. III. Title.
QB46.O762 2011   520—dc22   2011000306

Printed in the United States of America

50 49 48 47 46

This book has been officially leveled by using the F&P Text Level Gradient™
Leveling System.

For Wil and Melanie Aiken

Scientific Consultants:

STEPHANIE L. PARELLO, Astronomy Education Coordinator, Hayden Planetarium, New York City

HEIDI JOHNSON, Earth Science and Paleontology, Lowell Junior High School, Bisbee, Arizona

RICHARD McCOLMAN, Morehead Planetarium and Science Center, Chapel Hill, North Carolina

Education Consultant:

MELINDA MURPHY, Media Specialist, Reed Elementary School, Cypress Fairbanks Independent School District, Houston, Texas

Very special thanks to Dr. Alan J. Friedman, Ph.D., Director, New York Hall of Science, for his professional hospitality, meticulous marble mathematics, stunning photographic contribution, and unflagging moral support.

We would also like to thank Paul Coughlin for his ongoing photographic contribution to the series and, again, our wonderful, creative team at Random House: Joanne Yates, Helena Winston, Diane Landolf, Cathy Goldsmith, Mallory Loehr, and, of course, our wonderful editor, Shana Corey.

SPACE

Contents

Dear Readers,

We had a really exciting space adventure in <u>Midnight on the Moon</u>. When we got back to Frog Creek, we wanted to learn more about the Moon and space travel, and about stars and planets. So we set out on another mission: fact-tracking!

We went to the library and checked out books about astronomy.

We watched a DVD about the first men to walk on the Moon.

We found a website that helped us learn more about planets and stars.

Finally, we went to a science museum

and saw a great show about the birth of the universe 15 billion years ago!

Now we want to share the facts with you.

So get your notebook, get your backpack, and get ready to blast off on your own fact-tracking mission in <u>Space</u>!

Jack

Annie

1

Astronomy

People have always been interested in space.

Cave people painted pictures of the night sky on the walls of their caves. Ancient Egyptians believed there were Sun gods and Moon goddesses. The ancient Chinese built stone towers so they could study the sky more closely.

Over the centuries, people began to write down what they learned from looking at the skies. They gave the planets names. They made maps of the stars. They noted changes in the sky from month to month and from year to year.

Ancient Aztec calendar

The first calendars were based on changes people saw in the heavens.

The word astronomy comes from the Greek language. It means "naming the stars."

The study of the skies became the very first science. This science is called *astronomy* (uh-STRAHN-uh-mee).

Ancient Astronomy

Nearly 2,000 years ago, an astronomer

14

in Egypt named Ptolemy (TAHL-uh-mee) wrote the first books about astronomy. In his books, Ptolemy described how he thought the stars and planets moved in the sky.

Ptolemy (A.D. 90–165)

Ptolemy believed that Earth was at the center of everything. He thought the Sun, stars, and everything else in the sky traveled around Earth.

For over a thousand years, nearly everyone accepted Ptolemy's ideas as facts. They did not know that Ptolemy's "facts" were completely wrong.

Copernicus

Nicolaus Copernicus (nihk-uh-LAY-us koh-PUR-nuh-kus) was a Polish astronomer. He lived nearly 1,400 years after Ptolemy.

Copernicus
(A.D. 1473-1543)

Copernicus studied Ptolemy's ideas for a long time. He knew something was not right.

Copernicus figured out that the Sun does *not* travel around Earth. It's really the other way around! Earth and all the other planets travel around the Sun.

Copernicus was afraid people would not accept his ideas. So he waited until he was about to die to let the world know what he thought. In 1543, he published a book that said Ptolemy was wrong.

Copernicus's fears came true. People were furious when they read his book! They liked thinking that Earth was the center of everything.

For many years, it was against the law even to *talk* about Copernicus's

Oh, wow! Copernicus died just a few months after his book was published.

16

ideas. The few people who believed Copernicus kept their belief secret.

Galileo

One person who believed Copernicus was an Italian astronomer named Galileo Galilei (gal-uh-LAY-oh gal-uh-LAY). Galileo was sure Copernicus was right. But he didn't know how to prove it.

Galileo (1564–1642)

One day, Galileo heard about a new invention. The invention was what we now call a *telescope.* The telescope made distant things seem closer.

The first telescopes were used mostly on battlefields.

Galileo couldn't believe that no one had used a telescope to study the sky! He was so excited by this idea that he built a telescope of his own.

Galileo's telescope

When Galileo peered through his telescope into the night sky, modern astronomy was born.

Galileo saw rings around the planet Saturn.

Saturn

He saw moons circling the planet Jupiter.

He saw that the planet Venus seemed to change shape, just like our Moon.

Jupiter

And he saw that there were millions and millions of stars—far more than anyone had ever imagined.

Venus

The longer Galileo looked into the heavens, the more certain he became that Earth was *not* the center of everything!

Galileo studied the sky for the next 30 years. He wrote many books about his discoveries. Near the end of his life, he was arrested for teaching his ideas to others. He died trying to show people that Copernicus was right.

Sir Isaac Newton
(1643-1727)

Sir Isaac Newton

Isaac Newton was an English scientist. He made many discoveries. His most important discovery was the *law of gravity*.

Gravity is the invisible force that pulls everything on Earth toward the ground. Without gravity, we'd all float away!

Newton thought it was gravity that kept the Moon traveling around Earth. He thought the Sun might have gravity, too. That would explain why Earth and the other planets kept traveling around the Sun instead of flying off into space.

Theories are well-tested scientific explanations.

Newton's ideas about gravity helped people understand and accept the theories of Copernicus and Galileo.

Early Astronomers

Ptolemy

Copernicus

Galileo

Newton

The Big Mistake

Copernicus, Galileo, and Newton were on the right path to understanding space. But they made one big mistake. They all thought that *everything* in space traveled around the Sun.

Over time, astronomers have learned much more. They've learned that far from being the center of everything, the Sun is just another star among billions and billions of stars. And they've learned that Earth is a tiny speck in a universe so big it's almost impossible to imagine.

Jack and Annie Present:
Telescopes—Then and Now

Hans Lippershey (HAHNS LIP-ur-shay) invented the telescope in 1608. Lippershey was a Dutch eyeglass maker. Stories say he got the idea by watching his children play with lenses for his eyeglasses.

Sir Isaac Newton invented a telescope that used mirrors. A mirror makes it possible for bigger lenses to see farther without distortion.

Newton's telescope

Telescopes that use mirrors are called <u>reflecting telescopes</u>.

The *Hubble Space Telescope* is a telescope that travels in space. It sends pictures of planets, stars, and galaxies back to computers on Earth. The Hubble can see objects that are billions and billions of miles away.

The Hubble Space Telescope was launched in 1990.

The biggest telescopes in the world are located in Chile. They are operated by the European Southern Observatory and are linked by computers.

The combined power of these telescopes is strong enough to see a person waving to Earth from the Moon.

Hello, Jack!

2

The Universe

The *universe* is everything there is. It is
the Sun and Earth and all the other planets
and stars and all the space between them.
It is full of dust and rocks and ice and gas.
Mostly it is full of nothing—just trillions
and trillions of miles of open space.

The Birth of the Universe

The universe was born so long ago that no
one knows for sure how it happened.

Today, most astronomers think the universe began with a huge explosion. They call the explosion the *Big Bang*. They think that it happened about 13.75 billion years ago.

Two things happened at the moment of the Big Bang. First, the stuff that would

Millions, Billions, and Trillions

The universe is *huge*. We have to use very big numbers when we talk about distances in the universe and the number of stars in the universe.

How much is a <u>million</u>?

A million marbles would fill the inside of a small car!

become everything in the universe came into being. Second, the universe began *expanding*. That means it went flying in all directions, moving farther and farther away from the spot where the Big Bang happened.

The universe is still expanding today!

How much is a <u>billion</u>?

A billion marbles would fill the inside of a two-story house!

How much is a <u>trillion</u>?

A trillion marbles would fill the biggest domed stadium right up to the roof!

It is the open space between bits of matter that expands. The stars, planets, and other matter stay the same size. The universe is like a rising loaf of raisin bread! The raisins stay the same size but move farther apart as the dough rises.

The universe expanded *very* quickly after the Big Bang. At the moment of the explosion, the whole universe was smaller than the head of a pin. Within a second, it was billions of times bigger than Earth.

For billions of years after the Big Bang, everything in the universe was just very, very hot gas. As the universe expanded and cooled, some of the gas began to clump together. The clumps grew into huge, fiery balls. These balls became the first stars.

Stars and Galaxies

When we look at the night sky, we see just

a few of the stars that are in the universe. Even on the clearest night, only about 2,000 stars can be seen without a telescope. Astronomers think there may be as many as *10 billion trillion* stars in the universe!

Stars we can see = 2,000
Stars in the universe =
10,000,000,000,000,000,000,000

Stars are grouped together in *galaxies*. Most galaxies contain hundreds of billions of stars.

All the stars we can see are part of a galaxy called the *Milky Way*. There are more than 200 billion stars in the Milky Way. One of those stars is our Sun.

Some stars are smaller than Earth. Others are 300 times larger than the Sun!

Light-years

Astronomers measure distances in space in *light-years*. A light-year is the distance light can travel through space in one year. One light-year = 5,880 billion miles.

The Sun is the star closest to Earth. It takes light from the Sun about eight minutes to reach Earth. The next closest star is Proxima Centauri (PRAHK-suh-muh sen-TAW-ree). It takes light from Proxima Centauri about *four years* to

Proxima Centauri

Light—spends four years traveling through space

Earth

reach Earth! So astronomers say that Proxima Centauri is *four light-years* away.

It takes light from distant stars billions of years to reach Earth. By the time it gets here, the stars are billions of years older than they were when the light left them. So we really see the stars as they used to be! Looking at the stars is like looking into the past.

3

The Sun

The Sun is a star like all the other stars in the sky. It looks bigger and brighter than other stars because it is much closer to Earth.

The Sun is 93 million miles from Earth. The next closest star is more than 20 *trillion* miles away!

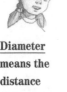

Diameter
means the
distance
through the
center of a
circle or ball.

Diameter

The Sun is a medium-sized star. It's about 865,000 miles in diameter. Compared to Earth, it's gigantic! Over a million Earths could fit inside the Sun.

Heat and Light

The center of the Sun is called the *core*. The Sun's core is like a giant fiery furnace. But the fire of the Sun is not an ordinary fire. No ordinary fire could warm Earth from 93 million miles away!

The fire at the center of the Sun is called a *nuclear reaction*. Due to its enormous heat and pressure, the Sun makes heavier elements out of lighter ones. This process releases lots and lots of energy.

The energy travels from the Sun's core to the surface. When the energy reaches the surface, it shoots into space as heat and light.

Energy

Heat and light

Earth

takes two million years for energy to travel from the Sun's core to the Sun's surface.

Core

Sun

It takes only eight minutes for the Sun's heat and light to reach Earth!

Spots, Flares, and Prominences

Since the Sun is a ball of gas, its surface is not solid like Earth's. It is always changing, like the surface of a pot of boiling water.

There are often dark patches on the surface of the Sun. These dark patches are called *sunspots*. Sunspots look dark because they are not quite as hot as the rest of the Sun's surface. Most sunspots are many times bigger than Earth.

Sunspot

Giant bursts of light and heat some-times explode above sunspots. These are called *solar flares*. Solar flares are twice as hot as the surface of the Sun. They are also much brighter.

Prominences (PRAH-muh-nens-iz) are

Sunspots and solar flares send out energy that can affect radio and TV broadcasts on Earth.

38

loops of fiery gas that leap out into space, then back to the Sun's surface. Prominences can last for many hours.

Most prominences are so big they could wrap around Earth more than ten times!

The Life of the Sun

The Sun is what astronomers call a *yellow dwarf* star.

As it grows older, the Sun will start to run out of fuel. Oddly, that will cause it to become bigger but cooler. It will also change color. It will become a *red giant*.

White dwarf

Red giant

The Sun will slowly lose its heat and light, the same way the burners on an electric stove glow and stay hot after they are turned off.

At the same time, the Sun will get smaller and

smaller until it shrinks to about the size of Earth. It will then be a *white dwarf*.

After it becomes a white dwarf, the Sun will lose all its heat and light. But don't worry—astronomers think this won't happen for another 5 billion years!

Importance of the Sun

The Sun creates our weather. Without the Sun, there would be no wind, no clouds, no rain.

Without the Sun, there wouldn't be any of the familiar plants and animals on Earth.

Without the Sun, Earth would be just a cold, dark chunk of rock in space.

The Sun is one of trillions of stars. But it is *our* star. It is the center of our tiny part of the universe.

Eclipses

Sometimes as the Moon travels around Earth, it blocks the light from the Sun. When this happens, we have a *solar eclipse* (SOH-lur ee-KLIPS).

The word <u>solar</u> comes from <u>Sol</u>, the ancient Roman god of the Sun.

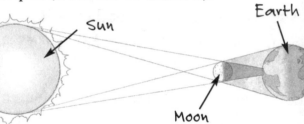

Sun

Earth

Moon

If the Moon blocks the Sun completely, we have a *total solar eclipse*.

WARNING!

Never look directly at the Sun, even during an eclipse. It can harm your eyes. Don't do it!

42

Many ancient people were frightened by eclipses. The ancient Chinese thought a solar eclipse meant a dragon was eating the Sun!

Total solar eclipse, February 16, 1980, Konarak, India.

Some of the solar system objects are farther apart than they seem in this picture. The differences in their sizes have also been changed. The artist did this so everything would fit.

4

Our Solar System

Our part of space is called our *solar system*. Our solar system is the Sun and everything that travels around it.

Birth of the Solar System

Like all stars, the Sun was born in a cloud of dust and gas. Most astronomers think everything else in our solar system came from the same cloud.

As the cloud swirled around the

45

newborn Sun, dust particles bumped into each other. They stuck together and formed clumps. The clumps grew bigger and bigger. Eventually they became planets, dwarf planets, moons, asteroids, comets, and meteoroids. These are the members of our solar system.

Our Solar System

Sun

Planets

Dwarf planets

Moons

Asteroids

Comets

Meteoroids

All the members of our solar system travel around the Sun in paths called *orbits*. The Sun's gravity holds the members of our solar system in their orbits. It keeps them from flying off into space.

Planets

Planets are the largest members of our solar system besides the Sun. Some planets are rocky and solid like Earth. Others are big balls of gas and liquid.

Planets travel around the Sun at different speeds. One trip around the Sun is a planet's *year*.

Planets also *rotate* as they travel around the Sun. One rotation is a planet's *day*.

Rotate means to spin like a top.

Rotation

Orbit

Even when we're sitting still, we're really traveling in at least two directions!

Dwarf Planets

Dwarf planets orbit the Sun and are round like planets but smaller. They do not have enough gravity to clear their orbits of other large solar system objects. Planets do. Astronomers are still learning about dwarf planets.

All but two of the planets in our solar system have moons.

Moons

Many planets have *moons*. Moons are large objects that travel with a planet in space. Moons orbit a planet as the planet orbits the Sun. The gravity of a planet holds its moons in their orbits.

Jupiter and one of its moons.

Asteroids

Asteroids (AAS-tuh-roidz) are space rocks. They are much smaller than planets. The biggest are much larger than an Earth mountain. The smallest are the size of pebbles.

If all the billions of asteroids in the asteroid belt were combined, they would still be smaller than our Moon.

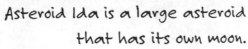

Asteroid Ida is a large asteroid that has its own moon.

A few asteroids orbit very close to the Sun and elsewhere. But most travel in a big group between the planets Mars and Jupiter. This group of asteroids is called the *asteroid belt*.

Comets

Comets are balls of ice and space dust. Most comets orbit in very distant regions of space. Only a few ever travel close enough to Earth to be seen without telescopes.

The Sun's heat causes passing comets to give off streams of gas and dust. These streams are called *tails*. Comet tails can be several million miles long.

Halley's comet, 1986

Many scientists think dinosaurs were wiped out by a huge comet or asteroid that hit Earth 65 million years ago.

Meteoroids

Meteoroids (MEE-tee-uh-roidz) are pieces of space rock or bits of space dust.

Earth bumps into millions of meteoroids as it orbits the Sun. When they enter Earth's atmosphere, they are called *meteors*. Most burn up. The larger ones can be seen as streaks of light in the night sky. When there are many meteors in the same part of the sky, it's called a *meteor shower*.

Earth's atmosphere is the invisible blanket of oxygen and other gases that surrounds it.

People sometimes call meteors <u>shooting stars</u> or <u>falling stars</u>, but they're not stars at all!

Some meteors fall to Earth without burning up completely. A meteor that lands on Earth is called a *meteorite*.

This meteorite weighs 34 tons. It fell on Greenland 10,000 years ago.

A few meteorites are the size of boulders. But most are just tiny specks of dust. Several hundred tons of meteorite dust fall to Earth every day. So when you clean your room, you might be sweeping up a tiny bit of dust from outer space!

A <u>ton</u> is 2,000 pounds.

Turn the page to meet some of the members of our solar system.

This way

Our Solar System

Mercury

Named after the Roman messenger god

Diameter: 3,030 miles

Temperature: -279° to 801°F

Mercury is the planet closest to the Sun. It moves around the Sun very quickly. A year on Mercury is less than three Earth months long!

Years may be short on Mercury, but days are l-o-n-g! That's because Mercury rotates very slowly as it moves around the Sun. One day on Mercury (sunrise to sunrise) equals about 176 Earth days. That's nearly six months!

Mercury is a dry, rocky planet. It has craters like our Moon.

Earth

Mercury

These pictures show each planet's size compared to Earth's size.

Venus is the easiest planet to find in the sky. It looks like a big star that shines brightest just after sunset or just before dawn.

Earth   Venus

Venus

Named after the Roman goddess of love and beauty

Diameter: 7,520 miles

Temperature: averages 864°F

Venus is sometimes called Earth's twin sister. That's because Venus is almost the same size as Earth. It's also Earth's closest neighbor planet.

Venus is really very different from Earth. First of all, it's the hottest place in the solar system besides the Sun. The temperature on Venus is more than four times hotter than boiling water!

Even if humans could stand the heat, they couldn't live on Venus. The air is poison! And it's so thick and heavy that a human being would be crushed before he or she even tried to breathe it!

Earth

Name comes from an Anglo-Saxon word
    meaning "land"

Diameter: 7,926 miles

Temperature: -126° to 136°F

From space, Earth looks like a beautiful blue and white marble. The white is from the clouds that swirl around our planet. The blue is from the water that covers two-thirds of Earth's surface.

Earth feels very solid to us. But below the surface, there is hot, melting rock and metal. The heat inside Earth sometimes causes volcanoes and earthquakes.

Many astronomers think Earth's water came from a storm of icy comets that hit Earth when it was forming.

The Moon

Also called Luna, after the twin sister of
    the Roman Sun god

Diameter: 2,159 miles

Temperature: -287° to 253°F

The Moon is about 240,000 miles from
Earth. The surface of the Moon is gray and
rocky. There is no air, wind, or liquid water.
There is a layer of dust over everything.
There is no atmosphere on the Moon to
scatter the sunlight, so the sky is always
black.

Since there's no wind or rain, footprints
in the Moon's dust will last forever.

The Moon's gravity is much weaker than Earth's. If you weigh 60 pounds on Earth, you would only weigh 10 pounds on the Moon. That means you could jump really high!

We talk about the Moon "shining." But the Moon doesn't really shine at all. It just reflects light from the Sun.

Moon   Earth

Mars is sometimes called the red planet. That's because the soil on Mars is full of red rust.

62

Earth   Mars

Mars

Named for the Roman god of war
Diameter: 4,222 miles
Temperature: -125° to 23°F

Mars is the planet that is most like Earth. Mars has mountains, deserts, and extinct volcanoes. Its year has seasons like our year. A day on Mars is about the same length as a day on Earth.

Still, Mars is very different from Earth. There is almost no oxygen in the air, so humans couldn't breathe. There is no rain, so it is always dry and dusty. Dust in the thin air makes the Mars sky look pink instead of blue.

Mars also has two moons! The moons are tiny—the bigger one is only 16 miles across. And they're not round—they're shaped like potatoes!

Potato

Mars's moon

Jupiter

Named for the leader of all the Roman gods

Diameter: 88,846 miles

Temperature: averages -234°F

Jupiter is the biggest planet in the solar system. It's twice as big as all the other planets put together.

Jupiter is called a "gas giant" planet. That's because there's no solid ground anywhere. It is a gigantic ball of gases and liquids with a hot liquid center.

Jupiter is covered with white, blue, and brown stripes. The stripes are really clouds made of different gases. There is also a giant red spot on Jupiter that's more than twice as big as Earth. The spot is a storm that has been raging for over 300 years.

Jupiter has 50 known moons!

Earth   Jupiter

Astronomers have named 53 moons of Saturn.

Saturn   Earth

Saturn

Named for Jupiter's father, the Roman
  god of the harvest
Diameter: 74,900 miles
Temperature: averages −288°F

Like Jupiter, Saturn is a gas giant. It moves *very* slowly around the Sun. One year on Saturn equals almost 30 years on Earth!

Saturn is called the ringed planet. All the gas giant planets have rings, but Saturn's are much, much bigger.

Saturn's rings are made of pieces of ice and rock that orbit the planet. Some astronomers think they were made by comets crashing into some of Saturn's inner moons and smashing them to pieces.

Uranus

Named for Saturn's father, the Roman
  god of the sky

Diameter: 31,760 miles

Temperature: averages –357°F

Uranus is a cold planet. It is covered with green clouds. Beneath the gas clouds are liquids, including water.

Uranus has rings, too. Its rings are made of ice and rock like Saturn's. But they are much smaller.

The most unusual thing about Uranus is how it spins as it travels around the Sun. Astronomers think Uranus might have been knocked sideways by a comet or asteroid billions of years ago. So instead of spinning like a top as it orbits, it rolls like a bowling ball. Because of Uranus's unusual spin, a night on Uranus can last for 42 Earth years!

anus

Bowling ball

Earth   Uranus

Neptune Earth

Neptune

Named for the Roman god of the sea

Diameter: 30,776 miles

Temperature: averages -353°F

Neptune is very similar to Uranus. It's about the same size. It's very cold. It has several rings. It is made up of some of the same gases.

There are some differences, though. Neptune looks blue instead of green. Astronomers are not sure why. And Neptune has much wilder weather than Uranus. There are storms on Neptune with winds over 1,000 miles per hour. That's ten times faster than the winds in a hurricane on Earth.

Neptune has thirteen known moons. One of Neptune's moons orbits backward! It's the only large moon in the solar system that orbits in the opposite direction of its planet.

Pluto

Named for the Roman god of the underworld

Diameter: 1,430 miles

Temperature: averages -387--369°F

For many years, Pluto was known as the ninth planet in our solar system. But as astronomers learned more about the outer solar system, they realized that Pluto was only one of many objects like it out there. Compared to the other planets, it is tiny—smaller than Earth's Moon. It also has other large objects near its orbit. Since 2006, Pluto has been called a dwarf planet.

Pluto is made up of a rocky core surrounded by ice and frozen gases.

Charon, one of Pluto's three known moons, is almost as big as Pluto itself!

Pluto

Charon

Pluto   Earth

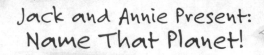

Jack and Annie Present:
Name That Planet!

Here's a fun way to remember the order of the planets. The first letter of each word in this sentence is the first letter of one of the planets' names, moving from the Sun out:

<u>M</u>y <u>V</u>ery <u>E</u>ducated <u>M</u>other <u>J</u>ust <u>S</u>erved <u>U</u>s <u>N</u>achos.

<u>E</u>arth

<u>V</u>enus

<u>M</u>ercury

74

Neptune

Uranus

Saturn

Jupiter

5

Space Travel

When astronomers talk about *space* or *outer space*, they usually mean anything beyond Earth's atmosphere.

There is no line that marks where Earth's atmosphere ends and space begins. But most scientists agree that anything flying higher than 100 miles above Earth is traveling in space.

Spacecraft

A *spacecraft* is anything that travels in space carrying people or equipment. To get into space, a spacecraft has to escape Earth's gravity. The force of gravity is so strong that a spacecraft must travel 25,000 miles per hour to do that. That's 12 times faster than the fastest jet plane!

Engines like those in cars and jets are not powerful enough to send a spacecraft into space. Rockets are the only way so far.

Rockets were invented by the Chinese about 1,000 years ago. They were first used as weapons and fireworks.

Rockets

Rockets work by burning special fuel at very hot temperatures. When rocket fuel burns, the intense heat forces hot gas out of the bottom of the rocket. If the force is powerful enough, the hot gas pushes the rocket off the ground, through the atmosphere, and into space.

Rocket engines work sort of like balloons.

If you let a balloon go without tying the end, the air rushes out and pushes the balloon away from you.

In the same way, gases rushing out the back end of a rocket push the rocket away from Earth.

The Soviet Union no longer exists. It was made up of fifteen countries, including Russia, Kazakhstan, and Ukraine.

Anything that orbits a planet is called a satellite—including a moon!

The Space Race

About 60 years ago, scientists in the United States and a nation called the Soviet Union began using rockets to try to put a spacecraft into space. The Soviets were the first to succeed.

On October 4, 1957, Soviet scientists launched the first man-made *satellite* into space. The satellite was called *Sputnik* (SPUT-nick).

Sputnik was about the size of a beach ball.

Four months later, the United States put its own satellite into orbit. The "space race" between the United States and the Soviet Union had begun.

Astronauts and Cosmonauts

Over the next few years, the Soviet Union and the United States trained teams of people to get them ready for space travel. Members of the American team were called *astronauts*, which means "travelers to the stars." Members of the Soviet team were called *cosmonauts*, which means "travelers to the cosmos." *Cosmos* is another word for the universe.

The first U.S. satellite was called Explorer.

Finally, on April 12, 1961, a cosmonaut named Yuri Gagarin (YOO-ree guh-GAH-run) made one orbit of Earth in a

Soviet spacecraft. His flight lasted less than two hours. But Yuri Gagarin will be remembered forever as the first person to travel in space.

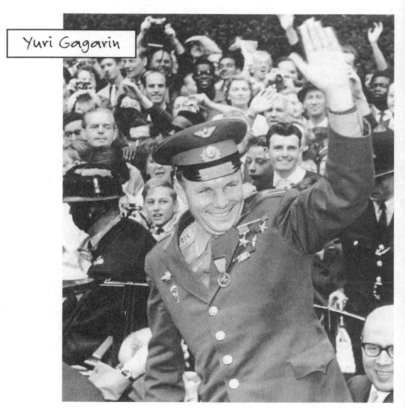

Yuri Gagarin

The President's Challenge

The president of the United States, John F. Kennedy, saw that the U.S. was losing the space race. So after Yuri Gagarin's flight, he made a bold promise. He said that the American space program would land a man on the Moon before the end of the 1960s.

For the next eight years, nearly 400,000 Americans worked to make the president's words come true.

President Kennedy said we decided to go to the Moon not because it was easy, but because it was hard.

The first flights into space were short but important. They proved that humans could travel in space and return safely to Earth.

Alan Shepard was the first American in space. On May 5, 1961, he took a 15-minute "hop" into space and splashed back into the ocean.

Alan Shepard

In 1962, John Glenn became the first American to orbit Earth. He returned to space 36 years later, at age 77.

John Glenn

84

Valentina
Tereshkova

In 1963, Valentina Tereshkova, a cosmonaut, became the first woman to travel in space. She spent three days orbiting Earth.

Two Soviet dogs, Strelka and Belka, along with 40 mice and two rats, were the first animals to travel in space and return safely to Earth. They spent a day in space in 1960.

Strelka and Belka

6

From Earth to the Moon

Landing people on the Moon was a much harder job than just getting a person into space.

A trip to the Moon and back would take at least a week. When President Kennedy made his promise, no one had been in space longer than a few hours!

There were other problems as well. In 1961, there were no good close-up pictures of the Moon's surface. Astronauts would need "Moon maps" to help them find a good landing spot. Also, no one had ever spent time in space outside a spacecraft. Astronauts on the Moon would need special suits to protect them from the Moon's very hot and cold temperatures.

American scientists and engineers worked very hard to solve all these problems.

A probe is an unmanned spacecraft controlled completely from Earth.

In 1961, they began sending *probes* to the Moon. In 1964, one of the probes took very clear pictures of the Moon's surface. The pictures helped scientists find a safe place for the astronauts to land.

Soviet Alexei A. Leonov took the first space walk earlier that year.

On June 3, 1965, Ed White became the first American to "walk" in space. He spent 21 minutes outside a spacecraft as it orbited Earth. He wore a space suit that let him breathe and protected him from the cold.

Ed White said that going back inside the spacecraft after walking in space was the saddest moment of his life.

A few months later, astronauts Gordon Cooper and Charles (Pete) Conrad orbited Earth for eight days. They proved that people could stay in space long enough to go to the Moon and back.

Then on Christmas Eve, 1968, astronauts Frank Borman, James Lovell, and William Anders orbited the Moon ten times. They wished everyone on Earth a merry Christmas from space. They proved that people could travel all the way to the Moon and return safely to Earth.

Finally, the Americans felt they were ready to put a person on the Moon.

Steps to the Moon

1961–1967—Probes take pictures

1965—Space walk

1965—Eight days in space

1968—Moon orbit

To the Moon!

On July 16, 1969, a rocket blasted off from Cape Kennedy, Florida. The rocket carried a spacecraft called *Apollo 11*.

Cape Kennedy is now called Cape Canaveral.

The *Apollo 11* spacecraft had two parts. Each part was called a *module*.

The first module was the *command and service module*, or CSM. The CSM would carry three astronauts through space and into orbit around the Moon.

The second module was the *lunar module*, or LM. Once *Apollo 11* was in orbit, the LM would separate and carry two astronauts to the Moon's surface. After they had walked on the Moon, the LM would carry them back to the CSM. Then all three astronauts would return to Earth.

Command and service module

Lunar module

There were dangers every step of the way. Anything that went wrong could ruin the whole mission. A tiny mistake could mean death for all three astronauts.

The astronauts called the lunar module the Eagle.

Moon Walk

On July 20, 1969, four days after the launch, *Apollo 11* went into orbit around the Moon. A few hours later, the LM landed on the Moon's surface.

When the LM landed on the Moon, they sent a message to Earth that said: "The Eagle has landed."

At 9:56 P.M. Eastern Daylight Time, American astronaut Neil Armstrong became the first person to set foot on the Moon. Fellow astronaut Edwin "Buzz" Aldrin followed a few minutes later.

Neil Armstrong had thought very carefully about what his first words from the Moon should be. When he stepped onto the Moon's surface, this is what he said:

"That's one small step for a man, one giant leap for mankind."

He meant that landing on the Moon was an accomplishment the whole world could be proud of.

 The astronauts left a sign on the Moon that read WE CAME IN PEACE FOR ALL MANKIND.

Neil Armstrong and Buzz Aldrin walked on the Moon for about two hours. They planted an American flag. They sent messages telling the world how beautiful the Moon was—and how beautiful Earth looked from space.

The following morning, Armstrong and Aldrin blasted off from the Moon's surface and joined their fellow astronaut, Mike Collins, in the CSM. Then all three astronauts returned safely to Earth.

Their mission had gone perfectly.

People all over the world celebrated the safe return of the three American "Moon men."

Moon Suits and Moon Buggies

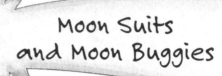

Astronauts used Moon buggies on three Moon missions. All three Moon buggies are *still* on the Moon!

Moon suits allowed the astronauts to walk on the Moon's surface.

Moon buggy

7

Space Travel Today

There were five more American Moon landings between 1969 and 1972. During that time, the Soviets kept trying to put cosmonauts on the Moon. They were never successful.

Finally, the Americans and the Soviets agreed to plan a mission together. In 1975, an American spacecraft joined with a Soviet spacecraft in orbit. The cosmonauts and astronauts shook hands. They shared a meal as they orbited Earth together.

The space race was over. A new era of space cooperation had begun.

In July 1975, astronaut Thomas P. Stafford shook hands with cosmonaut Alexei A. Leonov in space.

Space Stations

When they weren't able to land a man on the Moon, the Soviets began working on a different kind of space project. They began to build *space stations*.

A space station is like a house in space. There is room inside for space travelers to eat and sleep. There is also room for them to conduct many kinds of experiments.

An <u>experiment</u> is a test to find out or prove something.

Between 1971 and 1982, the Soviet Union launched seven space stations. All these space stations were named *Salyut* (sal-YOOT). *Salyut* is the Russian word for "salute." Soviet leaders named the space stations as a salute to Yuri Gagarin.

Space stations can stay in space for many years.

The United States has put only one space station into orbit. It was called *Skylab*. *Skylab* was in orbit from 1973 to 1979. It gave much information about the effects of long-term space travel on humans.

In 1986, the Soviet Union launched a new kind of space station. It was called *Mir*

Mir was supposed to orbit Earth for five years. With new parts and many repairs, Mir stayed in space for 15 years.

(MEER). *Mir* is the Russian word for "peace."

Space travelers from many countries visited *Mir* while it was in orbit around Earth. Some stayed on board *Mir* for over a year. They proved that people could live in space long enough to travel to other planets.

Mir was finally abandoned in 2001. It fell safely to Earth.

The International Space Station

Now several countries around the world work together on a new space station. It is called the *International Space Station*, or ISS.

The first parts of the ISS were launched by Russia and the U.S. in 1998.

Like *Mir*, the ISS was put together in space. It is twice as big as a football field. From Earth, it looks like the brightest star in the sky.

Scientists on the ISS do experiments every day. They are learning how lack of gravity affects living things. They also plan to test spacecraft that might be used on future missions to the Moon or Mars. The ISS is a great example of cooperation between countries.

The Space Shuttle

For many years, the spacecraft that took people into space were built for one mission only. Then a new kind of spacecraft carried people into space. It was called the space shuttle. The space shuttle was the only spacecraft ever built that could be used more than once.

The first space shuttle was launched in 1981.

The space shuttle took off like a rocket. It orbited Earth for up to two weeks. Then it returned to Earth and landed like an airplane.

104

Space shuttle <u>Columbia</u>

Parachutes help the space shuttle slow down after landing.

The space shuttle carried astronauts to and from space stations. It was used to launch satellites. Space shuttle crews sometimes picked up broken satellites in space, repaired them, then sent them back into orbit.

Space shuttle crews also performed thousands of experiments. These experiments helped scientists understand more about living and working in space.

Turn the page to learn about robotic space missions.

This way

Space Probes

Space probes are robotic spacecraft that are sent out to do research. They take pictures and gather samples. A probe can go to places where a human would not be able to survive.

Probes have been to Mercury, Venus, Mars, Jupiter, Saturn, Uranus, and Neptune. They've shown that Mercury has craters like the Moon, Venus is surrounded by acidic clouds, and the gas planets have strong, wild storms.

Because of robotic missions, scientists have learned much more about the solar system.

Helios probe

Shuttle astronaut Mae Jemison

8

Living and Working in Space

Conditions in space are very different from those on Earth. There is no air to breathe. The temperature can be freezing cold or boiling hot. Without the protection of Earth's atmosphere, the Sun's rays are very dangerous.

Spacecraft like the shuttle and the ISS are built to make humans as comfortable as possible in space. They have their own supply of air. They have temperature controls. They have hulls and windows that block the Sun's dangerous rays.

Weightlessness

There's one difference between being in space and being on Earth that scientists can't control. It's called *weightlessness*.

Astronauts in orbit feel weightless because their spacecraft is constantly "falling" through space toward Earth. Luckily, the spacecraft is traveling so fast that Earth curves away from it as it falls, so it never hits the ground. But everything inside the spacecraft (including astronauts) floats around as if it had no weight at all.

Weightlessness affects everything astronauts do in space. There is no up or down. Tools, pencils, and notepads float around them as they work. They bathe with wet towels because water wouldn't stay in a tub!

Food trays have to be stuck to tables. Food has to be sticky so it will stay on a fork. Cookies are a little bit gooey so there won't be crumbs floating all over the place!

Ellison Onizuka was the first Japanese American astronaut. Sadly, he and six other astronauts were killed when the space shuttle <u>Challenger</u> exploded in 1986.

Space toilets have seat belts and foot straps. They don't flush with water. Instead, they flush by sucking air like a vacuum cleaner.

When it's time to sleep, most astronauts strap themselves into sleeping bags attached to the walls. That's because sheets and blankets would float off a regular bed—and so would a sleeping astronaut!

On long space flights, weightlessness

can cause serious problems. Astronauts' muscles and bones can become very weak. So astronauts spend part of every day doing exercises. Otherwise, they might not be able to walk when they got back to Earth!

Even with all the problems, most astronauts say they enjoy traveling in space. Nearly all agree that weightlessness is *fun*!

When a spacecraft is orbiting Earth, the Sun rises and sets about every 90 minutes!

The Jack Files:
Life in Outer Space

Is there life anywhere in the universe besides Earth?

No one knows. But many astronomers think the universe is so gigantic that it's unlikely Earth is the *only* place with living creatures.

The SETI Program

SETI stands for Search for Extraterrestrial Intelligence. *Extraterrestrial* means "from beyond Earth." Astronomers in the SETI program listen for radio messages from space creatures. They also send messages far into space. So far, they haven't gotten an answer!

116

SETI astronomers use the Arecibo radio
telescope in Puerto Rico to listen for
messages from space. To find out more
about the SETI program, visit SETI.org.

UFOs

UFOs are *unidentified flying objects*. Some people think space creatures visit Earth in UFOs. But there has never been any proof of this.

UFOs are sometimes called *flying saucers*. That's because UFOs in stories and movies are often round and flat.

Space Aliens

Extraterrestrial creatures are also called *aliens*. Scientists can only imagine what aliens might look like. They make guesses based on the conditions of the planets aliens might live on.

What do *you* think space aliens might look like?

9

The Future

In ancient times, people built stone towers to study the sky more closely. Today, scientists are planning projects that could take people into space for a weekend vacation!

Giant spinning space stations might use artificial gravity to make visitors more comfortable in space. These kinds of space stations could even be used as hotels for tourists.

Space colonies might someday be built on the Moon or Mars. These would be like towns with their own supplies of air and food. People could spend many years in a space colony without returning to Earth.

A major achievement in space exploration would be landing human beings on Mars. Scientists have been studying this possibility for years, but there are still many obstacles to overcome.

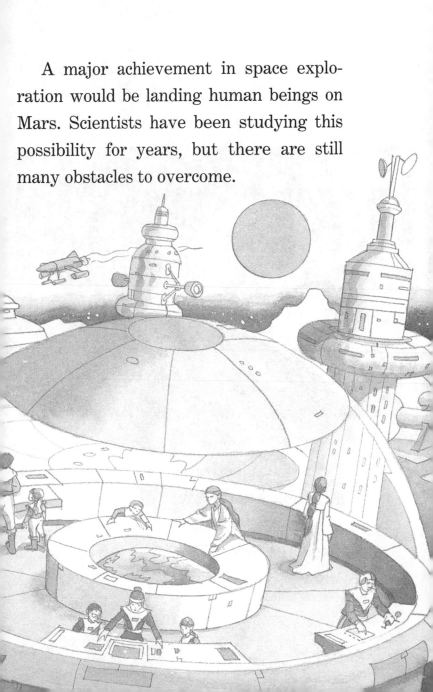

Who will be the first person to set foot on Mars? Sally Ride, the first American woman to travel in space, has an answer:

Sally Ride

"The first person to land on Mars [could be] a kid involved in a science project somewhere in the world right now. And it's going to be a wonderful day when that kid plants the flag of Earth into the red soil of Mars."

Who knows? Maybe the kid Sally Ride is talking about is YOU!

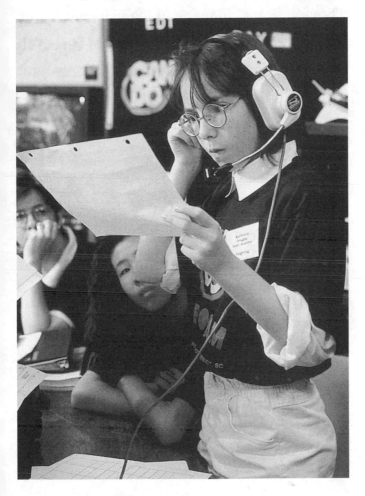

Doing More Research

There's a lot more you can learn about space and space travel. The fun of research is seeing how many different sources you can explore.

Books

Most libraries and bookstores have lots of books about astronomy and the history and science of space travel.

Here are some things to remember when you're using books for research:

1. You don't have to read the whole book. Check the table of contents and the index to find the topics you're interested in.

2. Write down the name of the book.

When you take notes, make sure you write down the name of the book in your notebook so you can find it again.

3. Never copy exactly from a book.

When you learn something new from a book, put it in your own words.

4. Make sure the book is <u>nonfiction</u>.

Some books tell make-believe stories about space adventures and alien creatures. Make-believe stories are called *fiction*. They're fun to read, but not good for research.

Research books have facts and tell true stories. They are called *nonfiction*. A librarian or teacher can help you make sure the books you use for research are nonfiction.

Here are some good nonfiction books about space:

- *The Everything Kids' Astronomy Book* by Kathi Wagner and Sheryl Racine

- *First Space Encyclopedia*, a DK Publishing book

- *The Mystery of Mars* by Sally Ride and Tam O'Shaughnessy

- *The Planets: A Journey Through the Solar System* by Giles Sparrow

- *This Is Rocket Science* by Gloria Skurzynski

Museums and Planetariums

Many science museums have exhibits about space and space travel. Some museums also have planetariums. A planetarium is a special theater that can make you feel just like you're outside under the stars!

When you go to a museum or planetarium:

1. Be sure to take your notebook!
Write down anything that catches your interest. Draw pictures, too!

2. Ask questions.
There are almost always people at museums and planetariums who can help you find what you're looking for.

3. Check the calendar.
Many museums and planetariums have special events and activities just for kids!

Here are some museums and planetariums with space exhibits:

- Adler Planetarium (Chicago)

- Carnegie Science Center (Pittsburgh)

- Griffith Observatory (Los Angeles)

- Hayden Planetarium (New York)

- Kennedy Space Center (Orsino, Florida)

- Morehead Planetarium and Science Center (Chapel Hill, North Carolina)

- Oregon Museum of Science and Industry (Portland)

- Smithsonian National Air and Space Museum (Washington, D.C.)

DVDs

There are some great nonfiction DVDs about space. As with books, make sure the DVDs you watch for research are nonfiction!

Check your library or video store for these and other nonfiction space DVDs:

- *The Big Space Shuttle*
  from Little Mammoth Media

- *Journey to the Edge of the Universe*
  from National Geographic

- *The Pluto Files*
  from NOVA

- *Space Station*
  from IMAX

- *When We Left Earth: The NASA Missions*
  from Discovery Channel

The Internet

Many websites have facts about space. Some also have games and activities that can help make learning about space even more fun.

Ask your teacher or your parents to help you find more websites like these:

- astronomy.com/en/News-Observing /Astronomy%20Kids.aspx

- childrensmuseum.org/cosmicquest

- kidsastronomy.com

- www.nasa.gov/audience/forkids/kidsclub /flash/index.html

- spaceplace.nasa.gov/en/kids

Good luck!

Index

Have you read the adventure that matches up with this book?

Don't miss

Magic Tree House® #8

MIDNIGHT ON THE MOON

The magic tree house whisks Jack and Annie off to the moon—and the future. Their mission? To find the last M thing that will free Morgan from the spell. Can they do it before the air in their oxygen tanks runs out?

Magic Tree House®

Magic Tree House® Merlin Missions

Magic Tree House®
Super Edition

#1: WORLD AT WAR, 1944

Magic Tree House®
Fact Trackers

More Magic Tree House®

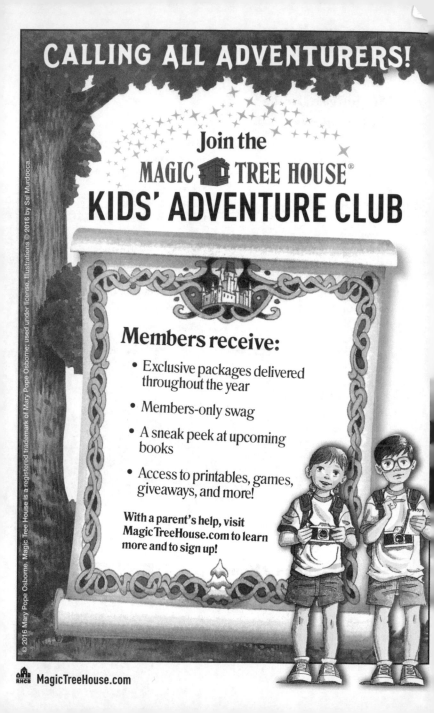